Full Circle

ISBN: 9798884757769
Imprint: Independently published
This edition printed 2024 Amazon
Copyright ©2024 Pink Sheep Publishing & Nicole Rosetti
All rights reserved. No part of this publication may be reproduced, distributed, or transmitted in any form or by any means, including photocopying, recording, or other electronic or mechanical methods, without the prior written permission of the publisher.
www.rosettipoetry.com
social @rosettipoetry
cover image by kirillslov

Full Circle

A collection of poems by Nicole Rosetti

Some from life, some from stories recounted by others,
some whimsical and some just poetic.

for my children

I. Inklings
II. Whimsy
III. Full Circle

I. Inklings

The Invisible Man

Sound asleep at Oxford Circus Underground,
a bench at Leicester Square
or simply west-end roaming aimlessly,
in a heavy enveloping overcoat
from which sprouted like a grey twisting Medusa,
a matted mass of homeless hair.
And just as aimless in the opposite way,
a time-knotted beard with a life of its own.

The force field stench that keeps his space
distinctly clear of passers-by,
the obligatory crumpled brown-paper bag
grips today's pain killer close.
His sole possessions we presume,
withheld from public view,
secreted safely in the voluminous pockets
of that mountainous, belted overcoat.

I wonder perhaps, if we had the chance
to lay those desperate keepsakes down,
a creased and faded photograph
of children, their mother, his life,
her sadness etched in black and white
and likely some time-worn trinket
he's long forgotten the meaning of,
but says that once, he was loved.

Spring Watch

A burning blade of light drifts
across the field this morning,
a solitary shard of sunlight that
lasers through broken clouds,
to set the grassy tips on fire.

The static parade of Poplar trees
lining the field's far edge,
show no sign of breeze to disturb
their towering rise from winters sleep,
to keep their sentry watch again.

The slate-roofed cottage nestles
at the foot of leafless woods,
a solitary watchman marking out
the gentle shift to longer days,
the spark of life in nature's bones.

The bravest blooms are setting out
their stalls by shaded hedgerow,
to mock their timid neighbours
yet afraid to show their heads,
as Spring stops by again.

Fanfare For The New Age

Every generation takes its place in time,
demanding its voice in history.
We're here to replace and we must erase
all that went before, until we fell from
a higher plane and must newly claim
our sage presence in the world.

All we know is that we're new and right,
the old must fall away to dust,
covers closed on ancient books,
new rules are now laid down by us,
more enlightened, more attuned with a
righteous grasp of beauty, art and song.

What came before should now be viewed
with accusation or ridicule,
our books written by literate clouds
set to music played by silicon machines,
where all our works will live for eternity,
all rise for the young, the new and the truth.

Downsizing

Today his car left the driveway
leaving hers bewildered, behind.
The driver, pleased with his purchase
drove away with a satisfied smile on his face,
along with a token of a stranger's life.

She watched it from the kitchen window,
listened intently to the rasp of the tyres
on the mourning gravel, a needless reminder,
each crackling stone spat out a sound
like tearing another page from a book.

Then the garden fell perfectly still.
There's a dry patch now, next to her car.
The emptiest space taking the place
of something substantial, entirely lost
in the relentless ticking of clocks.

The Purpose Of Dog

Sat in the comfiest chair, gazing out of the window at the lengthening day
and reading my favourite anthology of poets, my favourite works.
Across the meadow the wind blows a row of Poplars like chorus girls
practising their slender dance routine in perfect tree-choreography.
The new spring lambs begin their boisterous gathering, and suddenly,
as if a pistol explodes, they're off.... the *Lamb National* begins.

Anyway, back to the poetry, this is a particularly difficult line.
What did she mean by *deeply dusted* and what was the purpose of *dog*....?

A murder of crows appears, returning to the crime scene I suppose.
The lambs take no notice, they're figuring the odds
for the next race to take place and deciding its course.
I wonder why crows gather like that, a dark cloud of *ravenous* feeding.
Ooh! I must write that down in case I forget, these days it's so easily done.
I sip my warm tea, now what was I doing? oh yes.... reading poetry.

That's a good line there, the poet hits home evoking a shocking response.
But I'm losing the drift, concentration... something about a dog?

That really is the bluest, cloudless sky I've seen in quite some time.
Those cheerless crows would have to admit, even they couldn't darken it.
The sudden arrival of farmer with feed will get some attention for sure!
Every lamb joins in the half mile race to the Land Rover's open door.
Soon the action will cease, the dusk brings lambs and myself some peace.
Distraction fades, my gaze returns to the unturned page on my lap.

I start again at the very first line, now the poetry seems to flow,
comprehension returns.... Oh, I see! *deeply dusted*,
now it makes sense, but what was the purpose of *dog*....?

Four States Of Matter

The solid state of shallow youth-
atoms form the rigid bonds of
hormonally driven plastic thought,
randomly reacting, transforming
each word into something alien
to the untrained ear.

The liquid state of divergence-
of mind or body or imagination,
the perfect visionary abstraction
of thought and freedom of free
expression, of different, purely
peculiar, existence.

The gaseous drift of failing mind-
memory mislaid or slowly slipping
into the cracks of age, then to fade
into the frail fog in the agony
of the long kiss goodbye, to watch
their photofit dissolve.

The trace of ash we scatter
in a place that mattered to them once,
somewhere that makes us find comfort,
for that other life whose clock ran down,
where they're not really gone,
just taking a break from Earthly nonsense.

Safety In Guns

We've all heard that guns don't kill people,
that only people kill people.
Well, they seem to choose much harder ways,
a baseball bat or maybe a knife,
a machete, a hammer, a chainsaw
(If they're planning a massacre).
But they don't use guns.
Guns can't kill people
of course, only people can kill people.

Tanks kill people and maybe bombs,
though hit and miss or cluster.
Mustard gas, Napalm, spears,
missiles are guided, there's no hiding place
from a well placed land mine.
Fighter jets with Exocets,
laser guided hate,
but guns cannot kill people
as we know, only people can kill people.

We separate death-by-war from murder
and embrace a legalised genocide.
People are cleansed, never shot, but killed
from a distance by unmanned drones.
The dealer in arms sells fake ammunition
(since you can't *kill* people with guns),
so the victims might ask *how the bullet arrived*,
it must be derived from a human hand,
only people kill people, not guns.

The Actor

The actor wishes he played the fiddle,
the singer wishes she was a dancer,
people always seem to hunger,
for the something that they're not.

The writer rather fancies skiing,
accountants long for death,
dentists crave a sweeter tooth,
while athletes just want rest.

Sailors look for land ahead,
pilots lust for flight of fancy,
politicians stand for seats,
butchers roll a different joint.

Farmers dream of setting sail,
lawyers litigate for love,
doctors scan their future pain,
where waiters stand and wait.

Well, after all is done it seems
that wisdom calls to let us know,
all that's done and done in kindness,
is a life well lived, and some.

Restaurant Of Shadows

No matter the weight that's borne, no matter the force applied,
hate will always rise to the grimy surface of the human pond.
Hate can now be monetised, sponsored, promoted, cleansed,
a heavily weighted algorithm tips him hard against the grain.
Contrived and cheap to manufacture in his own dark restaurant
he feeds a ready following of hungry dinner guests.

He offers a choice of dishes on his menu of the day,
there's nothing free that he doesn't fear, or seek to eliminate.
Selecting ingredients critically he convinces you he's there
to protect you from the latent hunger lurking deep within.
He fights a constant conflict in his fear of something other,
that he fears may be inside him, turning critic's eye on him.

He has no power or licence, to serve his cleansing dish,
he stands alone, apart from reasoned argument or logic.
There is no bleeding artery, to disseminate his odious creed,
or cast his dish of acrimonious recipes to the world.
His stated hope of like recruitment, is catching the hungry ear
of any soul caught shopping, in his restaurant of shadows.

Religion, Love and Ghosts

When rivers flow up mountains
or mountains fall to earth,
when rabbit catches eagle
and fallow reaps the corn.

When ice is too hot to handle
and darkness lights the room,
when end becomes beginning
or blunt creates the cut.

When lie becomes confession
with bitter tasting sweets,
when kindness calls with cruelty
or freedom makes us slaves.

When gain is cast as losing
and sorrow cries with joy,
when noise is masked as silence
we remember to forget.

When all these things I witness,
I will cast all logic out,
then I'll believe in fairies,
religion, love and ghosts.

In Too Deep

On reading your deepest of poems,
I've struggled in scaling your heights
that lean so acutely on metaphor and simile.
My grip starts to slip and my tenuous hold
is lost as I stare at the page in confusion,
collusion evades me I have to admit--
I've no idea what you are talking about!

This poem seems to mean the world to you,
It clearly speaks to your darkness of heart.
I suppose it conveys you're deepest beliefs
and paints in the colours of your dreams?
There's room to assume it's your magnum opus,
your ultimate masterpiece, but I, I'm afraid,
haven't a clue, what you're talking about!

So I climb back down somewhat irate
that I spent an evening mountaineering with you,
stuck on the lower slopes of your peak
pathetically groping for tenuous connection,
for something, anything concrete,
a foothold, a crevice for fingers, but still,
I just wish I knew, what you were talking about!

Perhaps we have no shared experience
or perhaps it's me who's poetry-impaired.
Just maybe my own life took shelter,
from the versified rain that poured on you.
Perhaps if you leaked just a little
of your liquid line into my glass, you'd take pity
and *please, please* tell me, *what the hell you were talking about!*

Swallows

Pairs of swallows trace
twisting raffia tails
above the evergreen treeline.
It's one of those skies where
the higher you look,
the darker the clouds.
For whoever lives beyond
those distant grey-green trees,
It isn't raining there.
But here, it never seems to stop.

The rain soaked earth with fugitive pools
holds more than its share of the stream.
The small tall-gabled house looks on
in hope of the sun's return.
Its over-topped guttering drips
and splashes like tears
for the derelict Spring.
Enticingly close and desired,
the lengthening day descends
with the easy breath of new life.

There's nothing profound to say at this point,
no deep understanding or life-changing moral.
Just a soul at peace in a comfy chair
with a perfect view to the distance,
across a pastel green meadow
with evergreen trees,
and a gentle rain,
and what more
could I
need.

A Poem For The Passage Of A Pen

I dropped my pen, watched it fall toward the blue carpeted floor.
It only took a second to drop, no slower than a photon
hitting my eye or anything else that I couldn't measure.
There was nothing I could do to prevent its spiral flight,
a singular moment, embraced in the immeasurable catch
of a heartbeat, or a whisper.

A nonchalant missile buries its head into a window
where inculpable families sit to eat dinner.
Fulfilling its destiny, it latches home its hooks.
The dust settles like icing sugar on the disembodied limbs,
extruded from the remains, their lifelines run out
in a heartbeat, in a whisper.

A man who's fingers once danced on the keys,
in a whirlwind of music entrancing the crowd,
his skeletal hands now withered as his memories,
while his body decays, staring blankly out from a hospice bed,
where he breathes out his final number,
in a heartbeat, with a whisper.

Another ageless cry cleaves the silence of a room,
As the unspeakable fears of a mother are sealed
and she falls to her knees as she hears the words,
from the detective searching for her child.
A singular moment from hope to despair, visited there,
in a heartbeat, in a whisper.

In Hamburg, an elderly woman succumbs to her lung's disease.
In Chicago, a homeless man dies quietly, asleep, in the snow,
at Christmas.
In Paris, a small bird beak-plants a window,
mistaking it for sanctuary.
In the Amazon, a bulldozer rips down another ancient tree.
In a small by-passed town another store closes for the day,
for the last time.

My pen hits the floor.
It does that end-to-end bouncing thing for a split second,
then settles.
I bend over in my chair and pick it up.
The whole thing is over
in a heartbeat, or a whisper.

Quantum Entanglement

Just stop here, and listen.
Do you remember the last time
you stopped?
I mean, really, truly and completely,
stopped?
When nothing else could break the skin
of a complete, stillness.

So stop here now, and listen.
You might call to mind the
last time you lay down in
slow motion on your bed,
arms so still at your sides,
eyes gently but completely
closed.

Hearing nothing,
nothing but the background
hiss and hum of an all-erasing
silence.
Only the push and pull,
of your blood, hushed,
Pulsing.

When you couldn't feel your breath,
so low and short you wondered
If you might even be dead,
but for the gentle beat,
the sense of suspense
falling backward into dreams,
feeling it might last forever.

You know, that was my pale voice you heard,
a telegram carried on a whispering wire.
Those was my fingerprints left behind
that no longer carry my name.
So please, try as often as you can,
stop here now, and listen
and I will lie with you again.

If We Decide To Leave

If we decide to leave,
the birds we feed will still survive
as a species, their habitat restored.
The cats we feed will be feral again,
maybe the dogs revert to wolves,
the foxes go unhunted.
The sea will make a new appointment
for a colonic cleansing,
flourishing fish will taste fresh water,
as rivers turn their brown frowns
upside down and sparkle again
in their new attire, perhaps aspire
to flow to plastic-free oceans,
trees will not wonder *what happened to the axe?*
If we decide to leave, we will not be missed.

Sticker Price

The mother and children stand waiting in line,
the appointment now set for their interrogation.
They've filled out the forms and opened their veins
and finally, hopefully, today they will eat.
I'm sorry my children the oracle grins,
First you must pay to play.

The doctor will see you provided you're ill,
It just won't be today or next week, who can say?
Line up at the hospital, and swear your allegiance
to triage and trolley and corridor medicine.
I'm sorry my children, the oracle spins,
First you must pay to play.

Families huddle together for warmth,
as the new winter consumes their daily lives.
Feed the family or feed the meter, impossible choice
so they hope for relief or some grudging compassion.
I'm sorry my children, the oracle laughs,
First you must pay to play.

Nothing good comes to he who waits
or plays by the loaded rules of the game.
The oracle keeps them close to his chest
 and... well, you know the rest.

Missing

We simply must get home tonight
in time to catch the latest episode
of talent or reality show,
or moment in the sporting calendar.
We need to be sure we can hold our own
in the excited chatter and keyboard clatter,
the wagging tongues and ritual repartee,
of the office tomorrow morning.

We'll push and shove to board that train
and suffer all indignities, to breach the door
and for a moment ignore the news
that airs before our show.
It shows us true reality, unpleasant,
bloody, shooting-up with tyrant's needle.
where nobody is voted in, or out
and nothing is performed on ice.

How truly grateful we should be
to have such shows on our TV,
that divert our gaze from the realities
and keep us dumb and disciplined.
Heaven forfend that we should care
or raise our voice in halls of power.
Much simpler to avert our gaze
then cast our vote on eviction day.

Fugitive Monsoon

There must be, deeply rooted in all of us I think,
the tingling goosebump feeling when we hear
the sound of rain on windows, evoking states of presence,
centering something deeply ingrained in being human.

The sound well known to anyone who's spent some time outside
beneath a large umbrella, cocooned and safely dry,
while a light perpetual drizzle plays its dreary serenade,
a perfect circle of sanctuary, immune to April shower.

My day is seized and hijacked, sensing rain and heading out,
to sit beneath a bus stop shelter and wait there for the fall
of the first drops on the roof and the steady downward beat,
as my melancholic companion takes a cosy seat inside.

A rainstorm-music lover, I dive for the nearest cover
as the sky begins its concert with a liquid overture,
rising to full crescendo as the hardest rain I've ever seen,
bounces hard up from the pavement in linear crystal spears.

Evoking distant ancestries, awakening elemental root
intrinsic to humanity but ending all too soon.
Now just a simple pleasure, for the likes of such as me,
who fall entranced and captive to a fugitive monsoon.

The Great Idea

It slipped away quietly,
glancing all the time over its shoulder
to be sure that I was hunting.
It's still there, a somewhat ephemeral shape,
almost tangible, but untouchable,
teasing, laughing, just out of my reach.

It was a good one, a sound one,
intrinsically poetic, promising much
for a writer to mold into emotion,
in order to feed the hungry soul
of others, in the sister or brotherhood.
-- If only I'd written it down.

So now the chances of total recall,
are vanishingly small, even a sense
or pretense of remembering, a hunch
of a line by lunchtime occurring,
is incredibly small but at least, at least
I've thrown in some needless last-minute rhymes.

She Lies In Shallow Water

She lies in shallow water, eyes fixed upon the sky,
unseen by fishermen in boats who fish and drift on by.
Another rotting tree branch falls with a gentle good night kiss,
they search and searched for quite some time, she felt them for a while.
They came and went with boats and dogs but deep inside she knew
this soft, cold bed of mud would hold her closed against their eyes,
She will not move again.

Wind-whipped ripples on water distort the liquid light,
alone she keeps her lover's sleep, she know that this is it.
The cold and quiet trickling tide ebbs and flows again,
the rustling reeds make music for a lovers final rest.
She doesn't know who laid her there, no memory of he,
who lightly brushed her once-red hair and slowly loved her less.
Then told the cops she just left town.

Time will hide the smallest trace of evidence of harm,
the kids will soon get used to calling daddy's girlfriend *mum*.
Once a year perhaps a friend will stop to speak some words,
to say how much she's missed and float a small bouquet of flowers.
But he will never visit here nor let the kids play near,
his guilty heart, apart from fear will keep his distance fixed.
She calls to him at night.

She lies in shallow water, looking fixed up at the sky,
the seasons come, and come and go, still mark the tidal ebb and flow.
Time will have no meaning, her memories will fade,
the water shallow, dark and cold will not give up its bride.
The kids are grown and scattered now and he has long since passed,
there's no more flowers or words of love, just shadows drifting by.
Another cold case.

Media Studies

Katie lives in a two room flat
with her parents, two dogs,
two sisters and a brother.
Her father lost his job five years ago,
her mum is disabled, and can't work.
They scratch out each day with a visit to the food bank
and the occasional kindness of neighbours.
Once, her friend Julia
saw her standing in line at the food bank.
Her friends don't talk to her any more.
She hopes for a better future.

Julia, on the other hand, is doing media studies
and is currently studying *American Alternative Cinema.*

Katie's father hates to steal,
he wants to give his family small luxuries,
like makeup or candy, the little things.
He's on probation for Christmas shopping,
without any money or credit cards.
He can't look his wife in the eye any more,
afraid of the reflection he'd see.
Once, out shopping, he saw Julia
who crossed the street, averting her gaze,
To avoid the awkward conversation.
He hopes for a better future.

Julia loves her media studies
and just completed *Disney Studies and 3D Animation.*

Katie's siblings are younger than her,
she takes them to school on the bus
and helps them with their homework.
She bathes them on Sunday nights
while her mother sleeps off the wine,
slumped in an armchair they found in the street
while her husband weeps quietly in the kitchen.
Once, they owned a house, a car
and the lawn was perfectly mown.
They had hoped for a better future.

Julia lives for her media studies
and just started *Film making: Representing Reality*.
And sometimes, she cries at night.

This Free Course

This free course is free, of course,
no money changes hands,
a free exchange of information
changes minds instead.

It can't be studied in just one week,
a month or even year,
this course will take a lifetime,
graduation not guaranteed.

There is no class or lecture,
you self-study from the start,
your monthly course-work paper
will always stay unmarked.

Pay attention freshman students,
the questions will get harder,
the answers more mysterious as
the terms get so much shorter.

You will only get to leave this place
when arbitrary rules dictate,
so study hard, be sure and learn
each lesson feeds the next.

My Lips Remain Sealed

My lips remain sealed, there's no reason to speak,
your words remain locked in my skin.
A promise made is a fools mistake, no more
than breaking the trust and leaking slowly,
all the secrets of what, and where, and who.

So torture me with fire and knives and curse me
till I bleed, and ask me then, to give you up
and ask me will I swear, to keep your secrets
close to me, tied with ropes of guilt until stillness
greets the verdict, that the truth has handed down.

Confidence in confidence, breeds loyalty betrayed,
and blood from blood means little in the end.
What matters is the price of words,
the shape of love and the cost of grace.
So cut me deep and read the veins,
for you my lips are sealed.

Memorial For A Book

The rain patterns the window today
as the wind throws it across the field beyond,
viewed as though through frosted glass
while its sound drowns out distant traffic,
that normally accompanies this time of day.

Leafing through a book of poems by Cohen
entitled *The Energy Of Slaves*.
I've kept it close for fifty years while
we both yellowed and curled at the edges,
and came to better understand the world.

I recall it long-lost companions, *Flowers For Hitler*
and a couple of novels that no-one understood.
There's one thing I've learned about literature--
don't lend books, once they leave home
they never come back.

Of course I could find another copy to love,
lurking in the gloom of a bypassed bookshop,
but it wouldn't carry my blurred fingerprints,
the pages inside not so folded or foxed,
the inscription meant for someone else.

Not the same, not the same.

Half Awake, A Whole World Away

It's 4 am and dark,
so why are the birds singing?
If I went to bed so early,
how come I'm not asleep?
There's nothing on my mind,
so why have I been dreaming?
If no-one's there to hear me,
what is left to talk about?

There's nowhere else I need to go,
so why am I always leaving?
If such a thing as chance is false,
on who is fate to fall?
When time is traced in lines of loss,
why long for days to come?
When love portrays a perfect heart,
who here will sleep alone?

A Literary Tourist

Poetry is a strange country.
It passes notes to the voices in our heads,
from the intangible shades of teachers
or poets, reading aloud to our youth,
vaguely recalled, still close enough
that we can reach them, even steal them.

The Golden Staircase I climbed as a child
with Lear and the far away Jumblies,
still imbuing the same love of line,
lost in the deepest jungles of words,
that string out over decades gone by,
like beckoning lights on a distant ridge.

Yet this country has its share of troubles,
heroes, villains, revolutionaries and Gods.
We look for our personal meaning in their words,
in our fruitless search for vacant truths,
and dress them up in fragrant clothes,
that any fool can see right through.

Some are rightly celebrated,
for their brightly lit literary manuscript,
whilst snail-like, leaving a slithering trail behind,
illuminating the spousal suicides,
in the same kitchen, of the same house,
for the same reasons of doubt.

But of course in this country, that is no crime.
There are no poetry police to form a line-up
of the guilty, taking mugshots of those
who fall themselves as victims to their calling,
taking lovers on weekends, wives on a whim.
A strange country this, but that surely is its beauty.

Social Secretary

Regret is the voice she hoped was her friend,
who won't let her forget, reminds her on cue,
of the things that she's done, or had done to her,
the typist, insistently taking the minutes of her life.

Rigorously recording in indelible ink,
all the moments of accident, slip or mistake,
then reaching for white-out to cover the stain
of anything good to restore or balance the books.

The day she did *this* or the time she said *that*
and the right or the wrong, or amount of contrite
apologies offered in crooked faith, or defended in spite
of intention to rectify or douse the heat of a moment.

There's little she can do to unmake the past,
or try to re-write, or justify in hindsight,
seek to forget, retort or defend,
but in the end, regret is no friend of hers.

II. Whimsy

Stationery Love

Welcome my beautiful fellow addicts,
come, step into my compulsory closet.
I'll make us some tea and then we'll begin
comparing our office collections.

I'll show you my Sharpies if you show me yours,
We'll paint them on deckle-edged paper.
The rainbow colours reflect in your eyes,
like candy store treats for dementia.

The paper clips, stapler and scissors,
I'll swap for your blue label maker.
The laminator, folders and binders,
will hold us together for life.

Later, we'll go to the stationery store,
to stock up what we've already got.
Erasers, more pens and some notepads,
to record our increasing disorder.

The highlight of all these proceedings,
freshly served from my tape dispenser,
is just to remind us there's space on the desk,
for a four colour pen and a motorised sharpener.

Moon

Today you compared me to the Moon.
So let's unpack that here.
Apparently, you say I'm barren, rocky and heavily cratered.
That I only ever show the world one unchanging side,
hiding the dark one from view, and lighting the night-time sky
with an incredibly obvious name--
Moon.

Perhaps with a little more thought
or investigation or research,
you might have settled on Jupiter and selected a satellite there.
Ninety five lovelies to choose from, moons with character and beauty,
peroxide volcano with sulphur to spare, potato or doughnut shaped,
crackling with water ice and dense atmosphere.
I mean, who doesn't like doughnuts!

Names like Callisto and Io, Ganymede, Amalthea,
Pandia would be nice– you get where I'm going?
Orbits with a dancers counterpoise balance
in perfect choreography and tension,
filling the space with unmatchable beauty,
you could have compared me to Europa indeed,
encased in ice but exquisitely patterned,
but no, not you, you stuck in a pin and chose
Moon.

Infernal Rhyme

I guess I'm a fan of internal rhyme,
I fail every time I try to abandon
the use of a word, just because it sounds good
or sits where it should, in the scheme.

I refuse to agree, when people accuse me,
of using this construct too much.
But if it's a crime to commit,
I admit, that I'm certainly guilty as charged.

I'm even annoying myself right now,
but you understand how
it gets out of hand.
I stand corrected.
I'll stop now.

Pen Friend

A most beautiful line dances from this pen,
with animated surge that vaults the page.
Its bright blue script illuminates the tale,
in lithesome lines of elegant virtue.

It maps its path in pristine perfection,
and lays in the fingers like the hand of a child.
This pen may be cheap and laughably flimsy,
But this pen, well this pen knows.

As for this other pen, what can I say?
It staggers, drunkenly dragging the words,
leaving shards of indifference defacing the hand,
while refusing to engage in clarity or sense.

Just as the heart of the matter is reached,
it ceases emitting it's withering words,
forcing emission of verbal vexation,
Yes this pen, this pen is crap!

I know what you're thinking, you sceptical souls,
a bad workman always blames their tools.
and steadfastly refuses to shoulder the blame,
But just let me ask you before you pass judgement;

Is the writing conceived in the writer's head,
but the meaning extended by the easiest hand?
Do the words commence on the tip of the tongue,
to be finely deposited at the point of the pen?

This cheap, bendy pen (it was actually free)
may not be the prettiest, but it writes well for me,
and today, I need all the help I can get.

The Young Smoker's Guide Book

There's no better feeling than kicking back
after a hard days existence, than putting
your feet up in front of the telly, a cool glass
of juice or can of something gassy, and a
long, sweet, red-tipped candy cigarette.

While the boys relax and kick off their boots
put their stink feet up on the coffee table,
rummage in stuff-packed pockets with hands
that could do with a wash, then surface again
with liquorice pipe and coconut tobacco.

But let's suppress the appetite, for pleasures taken
on a working day, and fix our eyes on a greater prize.
Come Sunday you'll relish the ultimate reward,
when it's finally time for the one you've been saving,
savouring, that suck-ulent chocolate cigar.

The Heinous Crimes Of Vanilla

I stood trial for writing in tongues
and the jury confirmed my guilt.
I was told that the judge gave me life
but I'm pretty sure that was my mother.

I asked the judge to show mercy to me,
if I promised to make more accessible works.
I asked how I could appeal my sentence,
She said *try using more colourful words.*

Imaginary Unfriending

Only a child could imagine,
that a friend could be imaginary,
to share between us, good or bad,
some confidence or pleasantry.

To stand aside that other crowd,
who wouldn't understand our code,
with never a need to speak out loud,
our telepathic overload.

A working life, no time for friends,
nine to five for TV dinners,
weekends sleeping late, of course,
Sunday for the sinners.

Come middle age, full of friends,
those friends were simply full of it.
Too late we come to realise,
what's real and what is counterfeit.

So here am I, some peace at last,
friends scattered where life's wind blows.
The best of them are dead, or lost,
the static on life's radio.

Imagine that.

The Last Trench Of The Day

They think he was a fighting man who died
with his comrades on the battle's stage,
in the theatre of war.
His blood stained the pristine green hues
as his body flattened the tall stems
when it fell to earth.

They say he was likely just a conscript,
a simple infantry man of no consequence,
a life of no import.
He was buried where he fell with his friends.
He died of his wounds, the cuts they can see
in the skull, in the bones.

It's the last trench of the day to be dug,
the treasures so few for three day's work.
So they measure and log.
The first light he's seen for three hundred years
is fading late in the glowing autumn day,
as they cover him again.

All that remains in this English meadow is history
and a cool breeze that carelessly caresses the coat
of freshly turned earth.
The diggers depart, the experts emerge
from their huddle, pack up their equipment
and head for the pub.

Hopper

People who stare into nothing
without a thought in their minds
of any kind
in rooms with no connection.
People defining the word *ennui*
as *fallen between the cracks.*

Atmosphere seemingly sucked from
the room where once there was love,
or something unsaid.
Familiarity perhaps has bred contempt
for each other and what they once meant.
They sit trapped in the paint.

They never meet the others gaze,
for fear of facing decisions deferred
for another viewing.
The bankrupt eyes implore us to restore them
somehow, to reach in and save the day
or take pity and paint them out.

Wishing they were anywhere else but here
in this room where silence pervades
the vacant space between.
Knowing that time has fixed them there
we stand and stare at their shared despair,
just thankful, that we are not them.

Catitude

That cat passes my window every evening
about the same time, calling to someone
or something that I don't see.

It's mostly white with some orange patches,
and I blow cat-kisses through the closed
window in hope of a new fur-friend.

It stops, pricks up it's ears and turns
to look in my direction but with utter
disdain, just sniffs the air indifferently.

For a moment I think it's coming around
but it gives me the snootiest look
while twitching it's nose as if to say:

Yeah, dream on, that's not gonna happen,
but thanks for the use of your garden path.

An Amphibious Post

I put a frog in the mailbox
and then made my first mistake.
I waited for the postman to collect,
to see the effect.
He was very angry.
I was seven.

Time Writes

I began to write the occasional verse at the age of seventeen,
but a story takes a lifetime, for a lifetime's story lines.
The poems played with love and death, general teenage things,
in words from books as yet unread from years I had not lived.
We cannot read tomorrow's news before we write today's,
erase our past mistakes before we see the damage done.

And what have I to say to you, that you should listen, heed or care?
That I am older, maybe so, I may have more to tell than some.
I've travelled ways that should be left for fools who waste their share
of love and hate and things that would be better left unsaid.
A constant tight-spooled spinning wheel of coarsely woven cloth,
spins out to wind the threaded slew of years we have to follow.

So, what can I say to anyone, who has a latent tale to tell,
but struggles now in drawing out the true heart of the matter?
It's not so deeply cut inside or hidden round a corner,
waiting patiently for us to find the vision or the rhyme.
The secret soon we learn, is just opaque when we are young,
a story takes a lifetime, for a lifetime's story lines.

Young Lovers, Wherever You Are

She didn't deserve the lot that she got
so early in life that it cut her life short.
Children before she had outgrown herself,
not wordly wise and he more child than she.
It would be simple to apportion blame,
but suffice to say *hindsight is a fool.*
He should have known better, she should have said no,
but they made the best of it for a while.

Perhaps she regrets the way it turned out,
only she can say if her secrets slept well.
Life seems to have a way of creeping along,
preventing you burying the bodies you leave.
New troubles may visit in callous surprises,
when perfect lovers leave you too soon.
She seems to have settled, perhaps years have effected
some peace in her heart, though alone after all.

Slow Unscheduled Disassembly

I think I'll lie on my side tonight,
To see if that eases the pain in my back,
whilst I feel for the failing drum of my heart,
that just can't get the rhythm right.

My doctor says *you just need more pills,*
reaches back for her bright candy jar.
One for the stomach, two for the heart,
three for the pain, now go cat go.

It seems there's a silent slow-motion switch,
not subtle, from youth to here.
Too soon you glimpse through frosted eye,
the entropy start to grow.

If we were cars we could buy spare parts,
a kidney, a heart, something to re-start us.
Instead we head for a hospital bed
to die an undignified death.

A cat or dog we would put to sleep,
to ease their failing final breaths.
But we, we are tied to a hospital bed
to die in unspeakable ways.

Madagascar, Limpopo, Sargasso Sea

A treasured memory of a child,
an atlas balanced on Atlas knees,
satellite eyes slowly scanning
the world beneath my fingerprints.
Slowly tracing their silent passage,
from lips barely moving, whispering, dreaming,
Madagascar, Limpopo, Sargasso Sea.

Mandalay and Zanzibar, the Silk Road plotting
another course to who knows where,
or how I'll travel there.
From Kathmandu to Istanbul, my parents never knew
that one day hence I'd be far away,
they had no clue I'd be heading to
Madagascar, Limpopo, Sargasso Sea.

Timbuktu and Samarkand where camels make a home,
and Arab tents and pirates blend
as one upon Sirocco winds.
The wondrous dreamlike imagery
for one so young who knew,
all pain will fade in far away
Madagascar, Limpopo, Sargasso Sea.

Riveraphobia

It was barely a stream to be fair.
A trickle of water stumbling over
a gravel bed under overhanging trees,
somehow magical between two fields
it ran just beyond the sewage treatment plant,
beyond the pond with a thousand baby frogs
croaking in ex-tadpole jubilation,
fixed forever, in a child's imagination.

Closer to home, where the new road was built,
a passage to Narnia under the tarmac.
A pipe just barely wide enough to fit
a small child, almost upright, if they dared
to venture into the darkness and paddle
through an inch or two of muddy water
and finally make it through, not to Narnia
but the ditch on the other side of the road.

But none could compare to the towpath, that ran
by the river, from Eastleigh to Winchester.
Through fields, past the gardens of houses,
one with a model village on show.
A proper, full blown flowing river,
with reed beds and fish and a close-held horror
for those who could not swim, in case they fell in.
That fear of rivers we never forget.

A Question Of Rain

Questions, questions, questions
facing us these days,
the validity of war,
liquidity of food banks,
feeding third world nations,
failing to even feed our own,
heeding global warming voices,
chimpanzees for presidents.

Immigrants and asylum seekers,
poverty and crime are matched,
housing shortage, mortgage rising,
record homeless on the streets,
new pandemics fall upon us,
imprisoned poets silenced,
he or she, and who's to censor,
can we beat the Chinese to Mars?

Schools collapsing, too few doctors,
hospitals at breaking point,
Russian mothers send their children,
Ukrainian fathers shoot them down,
corruption stalks the halls of power,
money talks where fools don't listen,
third world countries fixed in famine
where harvests wilt in a blazing sun.

I stopped today and wondered this;
if all the planet's oceans evaporated at once,
tell me-- how long would it rain?

Murder Board

A body, strangely changed and corrupted,
motionless yet drawing closer, as though
attempting to show its assassin a face
that remains out of focus, but whispers
a name, something to remember them by.

Taking the decomposed outline of clues
on a murder board hung from its neck,
entirely encased in postcards and
post-it notes, photos connected by veins
of string and shiny push-pin bones.

The solution is closer than touching,
so you reach out and take the hand
that claws at the skin of your reason
leaving only your own fingerprints,
and a mirror to consider the crime.

In the quiet nights of endless questions,
the case grows cold and collapses
in tiny fragments of decomposed memories,
in a shallow grave you dug for yourself
or someone else, for some time later.

Friends

Let's talk about Friends.
Most people would say they want them.
Some people can't live without them.
Not everyone has them,
some have too many,
some have none.

Some are just too unlikeable
or lacking the social norms.
Some simply choose none because,
let's face it,
how do you get rid of them
once you realise who they are?

Some you know and love so young,
they steal away with your life,
and your big mistake is waiting
for some improbable resurrection day,
whilst you are a long forgotten scrawl
on an old discarded contacts list.

So let's talk about friends.
But not too often just in case,
we learn their secrets all too late.
Cast across the world we play,
and play too long and still we play,
a solitary game.

How To Paint A Portrait

I wrote a sad, sad song today, this is me
An open paper cut, still stings, it is me.
I told my story often as a lie, that is me.
I visited my pain on others, they are me.
Crows feet flew into my eyes, they see me.
The chambers of my heart fell dead, that is me.
The lovers counting time at my bed, for me.
Everything, everything, everything me.

The violin I played today, stole from me.
The poetry I wrote instead, belongs in me.
A steady stream of rain outside, called to me.
The bed I made in expectation, deserted me.
The friend I made in sincerity, rejected me.
The hope I thought was lost for good, returned to me
The reason for the all the years, made clear to me.
Everything, everything, everything me.

A fool who led the world astray, spoke to me.
An oracle of false information, lied to me.
I followed all the untrod pathways, laid for me
While others took the pavement, all but me.
I drank ten cups of tea today, this is me.
The unfriendly aches relented, they are me.
My catalogue of errors writes once more, it is me.
Everything, everything, everything me.

A Song For Three Ages

A song for the young is a love song,
every time.
Whether finding it, losing it or desiring it,
it's a hormone thing.
Either that or it's some romantic notion
about dying
of a broken heart, suicide or illness,
so long as someone is dead.

A song for the adult is a record,
a stylus stuck
in its grooves, endlessly repeating
the click
of a clock, counting out the days
of drudgery.
Pay the banker, pay the taxman, pay for
that mis-spent youth.

A song for the elderly is a sanguine song.
It's a been there, done that thing.
Time to surrender conventions and care,
let your grey hair down,
leave the night to younger bones.
Peace.
Content that the debt has been paid in full.
Flowers.

A Strange Day

There's a strange day coming
and I'm not sure how I'd handle it.
It could go one of two ways -
stay, or go, there's no way of knowing
right now.

It will be a day of discovery,
a show of strength, or a full collapse.
There will be an unsettling quiet
on the house, rooms will be closed,
clocks stopped.

There will be phone calls to be made,
a fear in the gut, life interrupted,
the points switched to a different track,
an unfamiliar station, and this train,
terminates here.

Perhaps it will be spent in reflection,
or pitifully probing for reasons why.
Maybe I will stoically ponder the ways,
of a world that grudgingly gives so little,
exacting such a heavy price.

The Hip Happening

Why is it that the older I get
the drier, toast becomes?
No matter how much butter I slather,
It fights me all the way down.
I can't drink coffee any more
though I drank my share in my youth,
I've long reached the age of tea
but bags, not pot, of course.

There was a time of Mescaline
the occasional tab or puff.
Now it's heart pills pink with sympathy,
to keep things ticking over.
Those Black Russian Friday nights
with the girls at the Jazz Room Bar
on Lavender hill, more distant now
than my close-held memories allow.

And getting up out of a chair,
what the hell is that all about?
A sequence of verbal extrusions
and a performance in three comedy acts.
But I'm staying up late tonight
Till at least nine or ten, I would say.
I know, I'm such a dissident soul
But I lived my share, you know.

Pretty Blue Pills Like Love Hearts

Perhaps I'll take four tonight.
It surely can't hurt to take more
than prescribed by my doctor's law,
the pretty blue pills, like Love Hearts.

For easing of pain in the head,
the red pills don't work any more,
but I'm sure it will be ok in the end,
to take the pretty blue pills, like Love Hearts.

To be quite honest I've never observed
a need to service instructions,
I need four or five (to sleep through the night)
of the pretty blue pills, like Love Hearts.

It comes to us all in the end, I know,
you can live all your life in good health,
till deceived by your heart you'll fall headlong,
for the pretty blue pills, like Love Hearts.

A Lepidopteran Life

I once was described
by a friend as a butterfly.
Not for my appearance
or short lived existence
but for fervently flitting
from one new thing to another.

She caught me with her description
of passion painted gossamer wings
that suddenly launch me into flight
when I'm finished with this,
enough of that, now on to another
new challenge or place.

When I'm done with this fine violin
this book, this brush, easel and canvas
that kept me amused for just long enough,
I'll flutter my new Lepidopteran lashes,
fly from these faded flowers and say,
been there, done that, what's next?

Run

The runner runs her race,
she has no reason to run.
The race just caught her up,
and her legs began to run.

Lap upon lap she runs,
seeming to have no purpose or gain.
Occasionally other runners join her,
and others drop out of the race.

Some fall exhausted from the pace,
some keep running despite their pain,
from injuries sustained in earlier rounds,
limping along at the back of the field.

Relief arrives as the bell sounds,
swelling of the crowd, sighting of the tape.
The pace increases as all else ceases to matter,
and meaning scatters from her view.

Her vision slowly tunnels in,
as the track runs out beneath her.
but there is no winner here declared,
each runner finishes at their allotted time.

The Memory Dog

If you're feeling somewhat lost today.
Can't seem to grasp what's before you.
If it all takes way longer to plan
the next half hour or remember a schedule,
or a meeting with a friend for lunch.
The years take time and care,
even pleasure and planning you see,
to ensure that it just gets worse.

Friends may say you should make a list,
others say little notes on the fridge
are better, you always seem to pass it
on the way in or out of the house.
Personally I would recommend a pet.
A cat could suffice but I'd put my trust
in a Golden Retriever, trained to retrieve
the things I forget in my golden years.

III. Full Circle

A Wrong Turn

I wish, so strongly I wish,
we could have stayed in Newton Longville.
Bletchley Grammar school, long since gone,
demolished to make space for the brave new world
called Milton Keynes, built to follow the Solstice.

Where the English teacher, whose name I forget,
since my fog of mind enveloped her face,
ignited the bloom in a rootless child,
and scraped a vellum receptacle
for her incantations, laying her curse on me.

A time of reading plays and poems,
words that fell from the page to the child,
fitted like skin, then latched within
and packaged with a course for life.
I wish, so strongly I wish,
we could have stayed in Newton Longville.

Bluebell Wood By Bicycle

A woodland awash with Bluebells and two small bicycles,
piloted by two equally small, mission-focused children.
Late in the year, the strange changing of atmosphere
hanging in the air, threatening the end of summer
and the cooler nights beneath blankets and eiderdown.

Their task today, to collect firewood to feed the stove
in the farm workers house where they live.
But they have personal tasks to perform before that,
in the small shallow pond with crooked willows,
overhanging the half submerged fallen-tree pier.

There are Sticklebacks to catch in the cane-stick net
and acres of Bluebells to explore, before the sticks
are hunted, mounted, transported home,
past the barn bloated with bales, inviting them to climb
to the roof, till the farmer's footfall is heard.

Soon, the winter will fall hard on the farm.
Frost-patterned windows bring darkening days.
Retiring to the playroom with the dressing-up box.
Outside, empty cages where the wounded, revived,
return to the fields now that harvest is home.

The Witch In The Wardrobe

She travelled to a stranger country,
stranger still for one so young.
She trained her slender fingers
on steel and wood and frequency.
She deeply breathed the poison air
until the Furies took their cut,
bestowed on her their mocking gift
while the stealthy Sirens settled in.

Slowly merging into fictive walls,
in her haunted house where the voices
called like friends to climb their
steep tormented stair.
With cast illusions born of smoke
they spoke to her of Icarus,
the invitation to her flight
would soon be sent to all.

No less guilt in retrospect,
a postcard in the mirror frame
casts silhouettes of disregard
from vacated hearts, each turned away.
Now what a weight the mourners bear
and what a price to pay,
in paler shades they hide their face
unveiled in masquerade.

Three Studios To Nowhere

I've spent years in a dimly lit studio
with the musical glow of dancing meters,
banks of buttons with hieroglyph marks,
faders that fade then rise again.
I've sat with the great and the good,
and the not so good,
and the really not very good at all.
But none of it matters.

I've spent years in a brightly lit studio
with paintbrush and oils,
turpentine, varnish and other poisons,
easels that support what I do to
canvases that take my picture.
Paintings that trot around the globe
while others still sit in the corner.
But none of it really matters.

Now I spend days with a keyboard and mouse
at this studio desk fretting
with pen and paper playing with words.
I put a handful into a blender
and try to make literary smoothies
that may or may not taste good,
that may or may not sell,
may or may not be read by others.
But none of it really matters at all.

Norway

A whole days sailing across the North Sea
on waves like billowing trampolines,
tossing the ferry, bow high then low,
vomit-inducing see-saw I vowed, never again.

Norway, on the other hand, was stunning.
Mountains, fjords, all the cliches
but real as the October sunshine
on the brightly painted wooden houses.

Autumn sun made washing in rivers
no less invigorating or painful or fun.
Coins with holes in the middle paid the same
in poker games, under canvas at night.

Camped on the road-side at the edge of a fjord,
struggling to climb the tree-bound walls
and charging, almost falling down again,
into the beautiful silence of nowhere particular.

Rhyming names like Levanger, Stavanger,
dotted the map and the mountain roads.
I'll never set foot on that ferry again
but I'd love to go back – by air next time!

Bessbrook

The Irish town of Bessbrook sits quietly
on a bend in the road, running down a steep hill.
On one side, the foreboding converted-mill barracks
rose menacingly from an industrial past.
On the other side a compound protected, encased
by a rusting corrugated-iron fence ten feet high
inside which various breeds of helicopter
landed, refuelled and departed.

All mud, save the concrete pads, solid ground
to save machines from sinking on touch down.
This place held no welcome for those indicted,
torn from the comforts of home and transplanted
into a conflict of shaky foundations.
They hoped their sentence would quickly expire
for the troubles they don't comprehend, they hoped
that their guns would stay slumbering there.

Most would come home a few would not,
fog bound wire-strike struck metal for one
that seemed to favour wretched men, observing
but not deserving of its grim misguided favour.
Most would move between the grinding gears,
spat out on expiry date from the dark heart
of the town that turned its gaze and grinned,
then called the names of the shiny new recruits.

Hill Head

Once in a while out of nowhere,
on entering a room I stop dead in my tracks,
as a scent in the air that suddenly
seems so familiar, morphs to a room
in a house in Hill Head, Hampshire
where the children of summer suddenly appear.

A back door porch with rows of Cacti
in guard of honour, lead onto a kitchen
with busy grandmother centre stage.
Beyond the french doors, two children
sit on a bench and soak lavender in
jars of water, in faint hope of perfume.

A day to investigate the vegetable plot,
have small square photographs
taken together, seated on the grass,
leaning on one arm and smiling on cue
for unknown camera in black and white,
in the small-lawned garden.

The affluent interior of rugs and wood,
with faceted-glass door knobs on each panelled door,
seemed still as the age it contained and quieter
still for that. My grandmother was tall and slender
in cotton-print dress, the essence of summer.
I can summon her sparkling laugh at will
and I often do.

The Snow Llama

I have on my desk two small reminders,
a toffee hammer and an ink-stained wooden ruler
that drew a line under a measured life.
When he died, like all old engineers
there is left behind an autobiography
in metal and wood, neatly arranged or hung
from hooks, hung now on different walls.

In silence for the absent hand, I stand
and look around this small, tidy office.
Nothing has moved, just as it was left
the morning he went to the supermarket
and never came home to finish the book
he was writing, too late in his life
to matter, a book that no-one would print.

I read a few of his unanswered emails,
the last one from me, that he hadn't yet read.
The one with a picture of a pet llama,
running through our village in the snow,
laughing at any attempt at capture.
I was sure he'd get a kick out of that,
but he went shopping instead.

To One I Loved

Those thirty years we spent together,
now seem somewhat unequally shared.
I lavished money and many hours on you,
addicted as I was to to the taste of your kiss.

Ok, you made me feel better at times,
kept my anxious heartbeat still and calm,
as I breathed you in like oxygen
then breathed you out again.

The only way I could break the habit,
was treating you as a human being,
to tell you I knew what you were doing
and to let you know we were done.

It took some time and different lovers,
who took up my cause with a different passion.
I never speak or dream of you now,
It's as though I never smoked.

Mystified

When Irish eyes are raging, best find some friendly shelter.
Look closely at the reflection to guess what you've done.
Stay passive in the onslaught, it's not your way to fight,
when you have no cause or reason, or desire to collaborate.

You know from prior practise that your unresponsive hand
will surely amplify the fury, and the damage coming down.
Retreat and wait for respite, arms raised and knees drawn in,
though offering only this defence, will enrage the Gaelic heart.

When youthful anger breaks the skin and lets a demon bleed
The jagged silhouette will always seek its easy rest.
It craves a broken target as a place to lay its hand,
and braver souls than you have met its eye.

When Irish eyes are raging, be sure that yours are shut
and rise above the conflict to a quiet, sheltered spot.
The damage done will fade away as sated rage subsides.
When Irish eyes are raging, there's a reason, it will pass.

Summer of '42

Like a rescued puppy it patiently waits
for my periodic attention,
that only emerges at a time to suit
my need for self indulgent grief.

A decade since and one more hence
the pungent paper will be turned,
the boys of summer will come of age
and perform for my entertainment.

Each cover's crease and tear is gained,
new scars inflicted on sacred pages,
hoping time has re-written the ending
where childhood dies in Vietnam.

This Isn't Multiple Choice

If you *want* to do it, don't do it.
If you think you *should* do it, don't.
If you're seeking *sanctuary*, don't do it.
If you're *looking* for love, then don't.
If you think it's the *answer*, it isn't.
If you're *sure* it's the truth, it's not.

If you absolutely *must* do it, then do it.
If your conscience *directs* you, do it.
If it's an *unshakeable* dream then do it.
If it defines *who you are*, you must do it.
If you've waited *this* long, just do it.
If you will *die if you don't*, better do it.

If it offers no reason, ignore it.
If it makes a difference, keep doing it.
If it brings you peace, embrace it.
If it causes you pain, forget it.
If the phone call comes, answer it.
When it calls your name, *that's it*.

Eye In The Sky

Spin, Spin, Spin.
we're only scratching the surface.
we've started up here and we're working back down,
but we're only beginning the cleansing.

There's so many species, mountains and seas
that we haven't begun to address,
frantically scribbling in our book of extinction,
they fall on the updated victim list.

Spin, Spin, Spin
from our arrogant heights we can spot imperfections,
we grind them out with our mechanised weapons,
or cull them until our target is reached,
so that nothing moves or breathes but us.

Rational voices shout into the wind,
of the world our children will have to inherit.
but it's not for a while and while the money flows,
we pretend that there's time to spare.

Plane To America

A one-way ticket, a solitary bag,
a dead-loss plan to never come back.
No point in lingering, all is lost,
no reason to come back here again.
January morning, dark as the ice
that leans on the frozen tarmac,
a cold, silent car to Heathrow.

Surprisingly quiet, travellers few, makes sense
I guess around this time of year.
I suppose they have plans, it *is* new year
and most travellers have travelled or arrived.
Last goodbyes, a letter is passed
to be read on the other side of the pond.
Checking in, checking out.

I remember I thought, when I saw the plane,
it was a little small for the length of this trip.
I found my seat, headphones on,
at last we start to move. I won't see home again.
Airborne at last, a lifeline run out,
that's all I can say about that.
Logan airport seemed a long way off.

They shovel us through the arrivals,
even fewer travellers here.
The customs staff are weary and keen to be home.
driving through snow that falls in feet in New England.
The following day, a similar flight
went off the runway and into the bay.
Lucky I travelled the previous day,
or I might not see home again.

Euston

Eyes as dark as the foot-weathered platform,
gaze transfixed on the grim space beyond,
behind are the fading, clattering wheels
of the train, that's carrying her children away.

That dread journey home starts at platform nine,
since the train left for Stafford and Liverpool Lime Street.

She's suddenly taken aback, by the absence of smoke
or steam, or other device to explain
what's caused the explosive confusion of mind,
and the sharp needle sting of the tear in her eye.

Blindly emerging from platform nine,
where the train left for Stafford and Liverpool Lime Street.

From the gloom to the concourse cathedral of light,
where reality delights to bite hard at her heart.
Can a station really be hated so deep?
Every child-stealing brick, rising up from the dirt.

Now that journey, alone, to atone for her crimes,
since the train left for Stafford and Liverpool Lime Street.

Past endless crowds who stand staring up,
at the furious clacking of cascading boards.
Faster and faster as though she's pursued,
headlong into whirlwind that's heading towards her.

Escaping the gravity of platform nine,
as the train heads for Stafford and Liverpool Lime Street.

The burnt, acrid air as the tube train arrives,
she runs down the stairs, then a couple of stops
to the urine-stinking stairwell, the blood red door,
the empty apartment, not home, any more.

Once more defeated by another's design,
since the train left for Stafford and Liverpool Lime Street.
Stealing her children away.

Room With No View

The Winner Hotel, I mean if a vision of hell
could exist in a building, well this was it.
Not the place you'd check into for a night
but the final refuge of the surrendered.
Five desperate floors of more desperate doors
hiding the lives of the haunted, escaping
the searching spectres of lives, lived out
in sunny Claremont, New Hampshire.

There's no use even looking on Google Maps
or street view to check if I'm right.
The building's long gone, I doubt even
I would recognise that town today.
But just for the time that I lived there,
just for the sanctuary granted to me,
those two tiny rooms in New Hampshire,
were home and I'd live there again.

Green Street

She said she new a guy who could get her started out.
A hundred bucks would cover it, three bucks a hit would sell.
They'd have to go to Green Street, they'd have to take the T
at night from Southie, worth the risk, but really, who could tell.

He thought perhaps that she knew best, after all she knew the drill.
She will look out for both of them, although he wouldn't take the bet.
A mutual friend who heard the plan, held forth some sage advice,
as he had made the same trip twice with a gun held to his head.

The train, still dimly lit and crowded, no-one met their eye,
people heading home from work or simply keeping warm.
A humid, rain soaked steam mists up the windows here and there,
the rattling, swaying car slows down as if for breath.

A sudden well timed moment, as the train comes to a halt,
the mugger grabs a woman's bag, just as the doors slide open.
Up, away and gone before she has the time to scream,
then everybody looks back down, at their paper, book or feet.

Destination realised and relief from stifling air,
a dark walk next, to Green Street, gas station on the left.
The street itself looks easy, suburban, clean and safe,
apart from this one, out of place, unkempt and menacing.

Once inside, some words exchanged, a phone call to the man
and back outside they huddle in the back seat of a car.
Driving now on stranger roads, they reach an intersection,
where another car from opposite, pulls up to where they are.

No words spoken, windows down, exchange, not even stopping,
the small square package handed back, they call the deal complete.
Home from Green Street, same damp train, no incident repeated,
he breathes a sigh, she knew best, after all, she knew the drill.

Home From The Range

Sometime ago, in my younger years,
I dated an American man for a while.
We went for dinners and movies, as you do,
around Christmas I seem to remember.

He told me of his life before we met,
a story book told with a wink of truth,
living a cloistered life on the range,
secreted remote in a cabin alone.

His task every day, was to ride the fences,
looking for damage and fixing holes,
and watching the cattle, would require
a horse, for getting around, I suppose.

He was now a single parent,
with a son, who I never met.
and he called me at inopportune moments
and read poetry over the phone.

I don't remember it ending,
maybe a cowboy wasn't my dream,
or, perhaps he just ran out of poems,
or reasons to read them to me.

It's one of those unsettled bills
that never got paid in my mind.
He was nothing but kind and gracious
and I hope he remembers me well.

Star Stuff

Who wants to go to Heaven?
Not me, and I'm happy to tell you why.
It seems terrifically limiting
to be floating about in an endless sky.
I'd soon get bored with cumulous clouds
and passing jets the only distraction,
with only a harp to entertain me
(and I can't even play the harp).
I'd soon be sent to the *other place*,
and I doubt even they would take me.

I'm happy to know that when I'm gone,
the Earth will not be far behind,
a few billion years give or take,
in cosmic terms, a fleeting glimpse,
when all of man and tree and earth,
molecules, atoms, Big Macs and dreams,
will retake their place in the galaxy.
Unremarkable dust in the cosmic device,
drifting unseen but with purpose and then,
surely, we will all be star stuff again.

Blame The Aged

I can't complain, I was young once.
Aged was alien and not of my world.
My peers were the people I granted
an audience in my youthful regard.

But now that I've reached this position,
elevated far in countless designs,
like years and experience and here,
it's the alien youth, I now observe.

They rightfully weep for the planet
but for some reason they blame me,
for every ill and disease of the Earth,
though my motives remain undefined.

In their cost-cut world, plastic is king
and the rivers and oceans, it's highway,
so blame it on me if it helps you to sleep,
Not that I'm complaining, of course.

I Suppose You're All Wondering Why I've Asked You Here Today.

Please everyone, take a seat.
My name is Dodo.
I'd like get a few things off my chest
and clear up any confusion.
So, firstly, to you...

I loved you then and I love you now,
and nothing in time has come close.

You, I never loved, you were unlovable,
and you never loved me.

and *you*, I certainly did not love you,
and your pretence of love for me
was a motive I ignored, but of course I knew.

But you, I loved you then,
and I love you now.

But for you, I would be ignorant of love.
love cursed me just once, and even though
each reminiscence adds another cut to the row,
I call it back, dragging its pitiful companions
behind and I quietly shed a tear and make
sure nobody can see that it's me,
remembering you,
and a lifetime gone by,
consumed by the memory of you,
as I loved you then,
I would love you now.

Thank you all for coming.

Hospital 96

Left home feeling fine.
By afternoon, I knew
It was the flu.
I stuck it out like a trooper,
drove home at five o'clock.
By six I had passed out on the bed.

The fever was so high,
the doctor said I must go
to the hospital right away.
They fitted me out with a hospital gown
I suppose they did tests
and then detained me for more.

Laid out on a trolley for hours
In the corridor, waiting
with others, snaking back
to the heaving emergency room.
No doctors on hand to administer
drugs, or opine on medical matters

Later that night, wheeled in
to a small, dark room, alone.
Later, an invisible companion,
a woman in obvious pain
who cried all night
but nobody came.

Medical to surgical
Back and forth,
ultrasounds, x-rays and bloods.
It soon became clear, they had no idea,
are you sure that you haven't been abroad?
Twelve days on and the fever was gone.

I could barely walk
when discharged home,
and they never found out what is was.
But it wasn't the flu,
That much they knew.

Me And My Shadow

I watched you today,
heard everything you said.
Embarrassing things,
things I would never say
but I watched as you just
went right ahead,
and said them anyway.

I followed you everywhere
just behind your left shoulder,
your personal Cerberus
guarding the gate to your mouth
destined to watch the many mistakes
I hopelessly tried to intercept,
in remaining fully complicit.

I could feel the words rising
inside you, to be broadcast
as though they were somehow
coming from me, how could that be?
I knew you would say them regardless
of any control that I could exert.
Now they're *staring at me.*

Full Circle

At seventeen I knew the future.
I could see the whole thing as clear as day.
We sat and listened to the music we loved
and shared as if we were joined at the heart.
The music played, we listened and I knew.

It's Autumn as expected, the leaves fall on us like
confetti for old age where we sit on that bench
in the embrace of the years, silently reading a newspaper
blown through time with news that we still remain
old friends, the frayed ends of a circle.

How perfectly strange to be seventy at last
as I wrap up for the weather and head for the park,
my mind takes a seat at our time, on our bench.
I always pictured us in our overcoats sitting with
me on the left. Can you imagine us now?

I sit and wait patiently, glancing down at the round toes
of the brogue shoes I wear these days for comfort.
We reminisce, what an innocent time it was while
the breeze reads back memories, slipping through the trees,
settling like dust on my absent sunset companion.
I have a photograph, that's all that's left me.

Broken Children

Youngest minds will lack the means
to process changing sanctuary.
What should be home and guardian,
can soon evaporate and vanish,
broken children's hearts avoid
broken daughters, broken boys.

Fathers who abuse there powers
to cauterise some childhood wound
inherited by chromosomes, and
passed in turn, with vitriol,
broken children's hearts avoid
broken daughters, broken boys.

Mothers lacking plain compassion
self-obsessed, oblivious to
the child diverging crookedly,
in open view with no recourse,
broken children's hearts avoid
broken daughters, broken boys.

For Want Of Correspondence

They don't have milkmen any more
delivering the daily pint or two.
Maybe a cold carton of orange juice
or fresh loaves of Mothers Pride.
So a milkman will not be knocking
on her door, to pay this weeks' bill.

Nobody writes a letter these days,
an impersonal email or text will do,
or maybe an instant message or two,
or a WhatsApp or social media post.
So no-one's expecting a reply from her,
for anything in particular.

She gets no bills in the post any more,
or late payment reminder or threat
of impending legal action, her day in court,
or a summons she couldn't ignore.
No need to make an appointment,
that she couldn't afford to miss.

So I wonder how long it will take them
to find her, and who might it be?
Family, friends? Probably not.
More likely the neighbours she never knew,
who on receipt of her notes of decay,
call the police who come knocking at her door.

Full Circle

Web: www.rosettipoetry.com
Social: @rosettipoetry
info@rosettipoetry.com

26.04

Printed in Great Britain
by Amazon